Classic Recipes of
FINLAND

Classic Recipes of FINLAND

TRADITIONAL FOOD AND COOKING
IN 25 AUTHENTIC DISHES

ANJA HILL

LORENZ BOOKS

This edition is published by Lorenz Books
an imprint of Anness Publishing Ltd
info@anness.com
www.annesspublishing.com

If you like the images in this book
and would like to investigate using
them for publishing, promotions or
advertising, please visit our website
www.practicalpictures.com for more
information.

A CIP catalogue record for this book is
available from the British Library

Publisher: Joanna Lorenz
Editorial Director: Helen Sudell
Recipe Photography: Martin Brigdale
Food Stylist: Fergal Connolly
Props stylist: Helen Trent
Designer: Nigel Partridge
Production Controller: Ben Worley

PUBLISHER'S NOTE

Although the advice and information in this
book are believed to be accurate at the
time of going to press, neither the author
nor the publisher can accept any legal
responsibility or liability for any errors or
omissions that may have been made nor
for any inaccuracies nor for any loss, harm
or injury that comes about from following
instructions or advice in this book.

PUBLISHER'S ACKNOWLEDGMENTS

The Publisher would like to thank the
following agencies for the use of their
images. Alamy: p13. Istock: 6, 10tr, 11, 12.

COOK'S NOTES

Bracketed terms are intended for American
readers. For all recipes, quantities are
given in both metric and imperial measures
and, where appropriate, in standard
cups and spoons. Follow one set of
measures, but not a mixture, because
they are not interchangeable.

Standard spoon and cup measures are
level. 1 tsp = 5ml, 1 tbsp = 15ml, 1
cup = 250ml/8fl oz. Australian standard
tablespoons are 20ml. Australian readers
should use 3 tsp in place of 1 tbsp for
measuring small quantities.

American pints are 16fl oz/2 cups.
American readers should use 20fl oz/
2.5 cups in place of 1 pint when
measuring liquids.

Electric oven temperatures in this book
are for conventional ovens. When using
a fan oven, the temperature will probably
need to be reduced by about 10–20ºC/
20–40ºF. Since ovens vary, you should
check with your manufacturer's instruction
book for guidance.

The nutritional analysis given for each
recipe is calculated per portion (i.e.
serving or item), unless otherwise stated.
If the recipe gives a range, such as Serves
4–6, then the nutritional analysis will be
for the smaller portion size, i.e. 6 servings.
The analysis does not include optional
ingredients, such as salt added to taste.

Medium (US large) eggs are used unless
otherwise stated.

Contents

Introduction

With its vast, open spaces, coniferous forests and freshwater lakes, Finland is home to a range of wild and domestic animals, freshwater fish, hardy winter vegetables and a glorious glut of wild and cultivated berries during the brief, but productive, summer. As a result of the challenging climate, Finnish cuisine is designed to counteract the long winter, with warming, hearty meat stews and satisfying soups dominating the menu. There is also a wealth of summer dishes that make full use of fresh fruit and vegetables, providing a year-round feast for all.

Left: The harbourside of Helsinki with the Cathedral dominating the backdrop.

Finnish Cuisine

The food of Finland has its roots in traditional country fare, which makes good use of simple, local ingredients.

The rural traditions that form the basis of the national cuisine mean that long, slow-cooking techniques, suitable for a farm oven, are common. This has resulted in a wide range of hearty casseroles and hot-pots, which combine the plentiful supplies of venison

Below: Baltic herring are available all year round and are a staple food in Finland.

and pork with root vegetables, such as potatoes, turnips, celeriac and carrots. Smoking and marinating raw fish are also central to Finnish cuisine, since these procedures infuse the fish with the smoked flavours the Finns love, as well as preserving them.

Mealtime traditions

Breakfast is the main family meal of the day in Finland, and it usually consists of a number of warming, sustaining foods, such as porridge (*puuro*), which is served with a pat of butter or some fruit or jam; wholegrains such as muesli, bran and other cereals, served with yogurt or fermented soured milk (*villi*); and open sandwiches topped with butter and a variety of savoury foods, such as cheese or cold meats.

Lunch is often a light meal, consisting of a sandwich or a salad. Dinner is usually a hot meal, served with a selection of vegetables. Baked vegetable puddings (*laatikko*), often made from

carrots, potato or swede (rutabaga) are a particular Finnish speciality. Creamy fruit desserts are popular, and vary according to what is in season.

The coffee table

Finns traditionally bake very good bread. Dark, rye and barley loaves are a major part of the diet. However, it is the sweet breads, such as *pulla*, the cardamom-scented, braided sweet bread, and the extravagance of the coffee table offerings, that showcase Finnish baking.

The Finnish coffee table involves more than a few sandwiches, cookies or a piece of cake – it is an important event that marks birthdays, anniversaries, weddings, christenings and funerals. Particularly splendid coffee tables are called for at Christmas and Easter, or to honour a special guest.

Right: Fresh pastries, such as these pretzels, form a major part of the Finnish coffee table.

Finnish Food and Festivals

Finnish festivals and holidays provide an opportunity for time out to observe traditional rites, socialize, share meals and have fun. Most of Finland's holidays are religious in origin, the exceptions being May Day, Midsummer's Day and Independence Day, which falls on December 6.

Easter (Pääsiäinen)

The Orthodox Church celebrates Easter on a grand scale and, although Finland follows the western church calendar, some Orthodox influences can be seen across

Below: Mead and doughnuts are served on May Day.

the country. These include the lighting of bonfires and, in western Finland, children dressing as witches and going from house to house to collect sweets or candies. Traditional dishes include *kulitsa*, a yeast pudding that is eaten to mark the end of Lent, and *mämmi*, a rye flour pudding, flavoured with malt and orange, which is boiled, then creamed and baked in baskets.

May Day (Vappu)

This long-awaited day, on April 30, heralds the beginning of spring, an event that is a cause for a major celebration. *Sima* and *tippaleivat*, May Day mead and doughnuts, are usually on offer. As with most feast days in Finland, the real celebration happens the evening before, on Walpurgis night, when bonfires are lit, ostensibly to scare off witches, in a similar way to Hallowe'en. These bonfire and witch associations were originally brought from northern Germany to Finland by

Above: A young girl dresses as a witch at Easter.

early settlers, and have now become an integral part of the spring celebration.

Midsummer's Day (Juhannus)

This celebration of the longest day of the year is a time for more bonfires and celebrations. Juhannus means "the feast of John the Baptist", an event that is celebrated across many other European countries, with bonfires, singing, dancing and drinking.

The connection with the saint is, however, coincidental, and it is the summer solstice that is at the heart of the celebrations in Finland.

Held on the Saturday closest to the actual day of the solstice, Juhannus is normally a countryside occasion, with most Finns decamping from cities to find a lake or seaside party. Birch branches and flowers are brought inside to decorate homes, and many people will erect a pole, like a Maypole, with the same pagan fertility associations.

Juhannus is also the Finnish flag day. Flags are raised at six o'clock in the evening on Midsummer's Eve and lowered at nine o'clock the following evening.

Independence Day (Itsenäisyyspäivä)

The day Finland declared independence from Russia is marked on December 6. It is a social, rather than traditional, celebration, and involves processions, flag-

waving and grand gatherings at the Presidential palace. It is a day for blue and white, Finland's national colours, and the lighting of candles.

Christmas (Joulu)

A period of cheer during the long months of almost unbroken night, Christmas is a festival of light and warmth in Finland. The main celebration occurs on Christmas Eve: at noon the President declares "Christmas peace" from the town of Turku. Christmas dinner is eaten early in the evening and children are

Above: Traditionally, straw decorations are hung in Finnish homes at Christmas.

visited by Father Christmas after the meal. Families gather to light candles and put up straw decorations around the house. The traditional main meal includes a baked ham with cold salads and rice pudding to follow. Christmas Day itself is a quieter and more reflective occasion.

The New Year is marked in much the same way as it is in the rest of the world, with fireworks and general revelry.

Classic Ingredients

Finns make good use of a wide range of familiar ingredients, as well as some more specialized foods that help to make Finnish cuisine so unique.

Domestic and wild meat
Pork is the mainstay of many Finnish meals. At one time, every farmhouse kept a couple of pigs to eat the household scraps. Practical and versatile, the entire pork carcass was used, with fresh cuts, sausages, preserved hams and many different charcuterie items made from the odds and ends. Traditionally, a pork chop

Below: Reindeer is a popular meat throughout Finland.

was served with a mound of crayfish tails and some dill in late summer, then, in winter, ham was the centrepiece of Finland's Christmas feast.

Beef has also played an important part in the national diet. Traditional slow-cooking techniques suit the meat perfectly. It is also frequently minced (ground) and used to make meatballs or a meat sauce, mixed with vegetables such as potato to make pies and pasties, or served almost raw as steak tartare.

When it comes to wild meat Finns are spoilt for choice. Elk (moose) are big beasts that roam large parts of Finland. The elk-hunting season begins in late September, so those with a hunting permit are able to shoot their own dinner. The carcasses produce large joints of dark, well-flavoured red meat. Both heart and liver can also be eaten.

Reindeer (caribou) have dark meat, similar to beef, but less fatty and gelatinous than that of elk. In Finland, all the offal from reindeer is used as well as its meat, so reindeer liver and reindeer tongue are popular. The meat from these animals is routinely smoked and sold as charcuterie – delicious with new potatoes and salad. In addition to the larger beasts, hares and game birds are widely eaten, both stewed or roasted.

Fish
With two gulfs, the Baltic Sea, hundreds of rivers and tens of thousands of lakes in Finland, it is little wonder that catching and consuming fish is a national passion. Common ways of preparing fish include salting, hot- and cold-smoking, and baking in paper. Pies, pasties, and chowders are also eaten.

The most popular varieties of fish are vendace, burbot, pike and perch, as well as salmon. Vendace, or muikku, are small fish, the size of anchovies, which are generally eaten whole.

Right: Salmon fillets slowly smoking over hot embers.

Above: Wild and farmed salmon is used to make gravlax.

Burbot is quite similar to monkfish, although monkfish has slightly firmer flesh. Finnish burbot live at the bottom of lakes and are prized as much for their exquisite livers and roe as their succulent white flesh.

Pike and perch are dry-fleshed fish. Carp is a good alternative, otherwise, a firm-fleshed fish, such as hake, can be used. Pike-perch, a member of the perch family, can be used as a substitute for perch.

Farmed and wild salmon are among the most popular fish in Finland, and are used in a great many recipes, including soups, pies, bakes and to make gravlax.

Fruit

The wild berries of Finland are one of the most spectacular food resources. Many of the berries, like strawberries and raspberries, are widely available, while others, such as Arctic cloudberries and lingonberries, may be harder to find outside Finland.

As well as the soft berries, rowan berries, buckthorn, juniper berries, rose hips and arctic bramble are also used to flavour stews, or are preserved in jams and jellies. Lingonberries grow in dark, peaty forest areas from July to October. They are very high in pectin and contain good levels of citric acid, which protects them from mould and rot. They make excellent jams, jellies and a delicious after-dinner liqueur. Cranberries are a good substitute.

Bilberries (wild blueberries) are common on moorland or in high, wild places. They are smaller than cultivated blueberries, and have a more concentrated flavour. Sweet and delicious, they provide

Above: Blueberries are a frequent addition to desserts.

the perfect excuse for a late-summer foraging expedition.

European wild cranberries are slightly smaller than their North American cousins and in Finland they are found in boggy marshlands. When ripe, the berries are red and juicy. They taste quite sharp, but this tartness diminishes after the first frost, so they are often gathered in late autumn.

Arctic cloudberries grow in much of Finland but are most abundant in Lapland. They are yellow-orange in colour, with the appearance and texture of raspberries, but with seeds on the inside rather than the outside of the fruit. Cloudberry jam is available in specialist stores and it is a good alternative to fresh berries in mousses and sweet sauces. *Lakka* is a sweet liqueur made from cloudberries, and this can also be used in desserts that call for the berries.

Vegetables

The severe climate limits the range of vegetables that can be successfully grown in Finland. Root vegetables are, perhaps unsurprisingly, the common staples. They are stored in barns for winter and feature in many traditional recipes,

Below: Root vegetables add depth and flavour to stews.

including stews, mashes and slow-cooked dishes. Among the types on offer are swede (rutabaga), carrots, parsnips, celeriac, beetroot (beet) and, of course, potatoes.

Potatoes are the national favourite. *Lapin puikula*, yellow Finn potatoes, come from Lapland. These small, long potatoes have a floury texture and yellow flesh, and are the traditional accompaniment to Sami reindeer stews.

Dairy produce

Finland offers some of the best dairy produce in the world in terms of quality, purity and taste. Finns have always drunk plenty of milk and it is common to see people drink a pint with their meal. There are many different types of milk available, including skimmed, semi-skimmed (low-fat) and full-fat (whole) milk, as well as buttermilk and curd milk (viili). Beesting milk, the rich, creamy milk produced by a cow after calving, is used to make a delicious pudding called *uunijuusto*.

Cream products include smetana, a high-fat, sour-tasting cream originally brought over from Russia; crème fraîche; clotted buffalo cream; and a curd cream, *kermaviili*.

The thriving cheese-making industry in Finland has been making excellent cheese since the 13th century. These include *juustoleipa*, an unusual baked cheese originally made from reindeer milk in northern Finland, and *lappi*, a semi-soft cheese from Lapland that is used in recipes and for melting. *Finlandia Swiss* is a sharp, rindless cheese, similar in taste to Swiss Emmenthal.

Below: Clotted buffalo cream is a popular dairy product.

Baltic Delights

The spellbinding landscape of Finland is dominated by more than 180,00 lakes and 175,000 islands with vast expanses of unspoilt boreal forests. Wild meat, berries, root vegetables and freshwater fish abound and, combined with traditional cooking methods such as baking, casseroling and pickling, have resulted in a healthy, hearty and seasonal cuisine.

The recipes that follow – from Cep Mushroom Soup and Trout with Cucumber and Horseradish, to Elk and Celeriac Casserole and Cloudberry Mousse – all play tribute to this distinguished heritage.

Left: Hearty casseroles are a major feature in the daily diet during the long winter months in Finland.

Rustic Pea Soup with Pig's Trotter Hernekeitto

Serves 4

200g/7oz dried peas
1.5 litres/2½ pints/6¼ cups water
1 pig's trotter, split lengthways
200g/7oz smoked bacon, diced
1 onion, chopped
1 carrot, chopped
1 leek, chopped
2.5ml/½ tsp ground allspice
2.5ml/½ tsp dried marjoram
30ml/2 tbsp Swedish, German or
    Dijon mustard
salt and ground black pepper

1 Soak the peas overnight in plenty of cold water. The next day, rinse and put the peas in a pan with the water, pig's trotter, bacon, onion, carrot, leek and allspice.

2 Bring the liquid to the boil. Skim away any foam that rises, then lower the heat, cover and simmer for about 2 hours, until the meat and vegetables are tender. If the soup has thickened too much to your taste, dilute it with a little extra water.

3 Lift out the trotter and cut away the meat, discarding the bones and gristle. Return the meat to the soup and add the dried marjoram and mustard. Taste for seasoning and add salt if needed. Pour into individual serving bowls and serve hot.

Flavoursome and warming, this pea soup is a good defence against the cold. With a chunk of bread it makes a fine lunch. The use of a pig's trotter demonstrates the Finn's thriftiness, ensuring that no part of the animal goes to waste, and it also adds a richness to the finished dish.

Hasselback Potatoes Hasselbackan perunat

Serves 4

4 large potatoes
75g/3oz/6 tbsp butter
45ml/3 tbsp olive oil
50g/2oz/1 cup fine fresh
    breadcrumbs
50g/2oz/⅔ cup grated Parmesan
    cheese
salt and ground black pepper

1 Preheat the oven to 200°C/400°F/Gas 6. Peel the potatoes then – and this is the crucial part – cut them widthways, not lengthways, down to three-quarters of their depth at 3mm/⅛in intervals, preferably at a slight angle.

2 Wash the potatoes in cold water then arrange, cut sides uppermost, in a deep, ovenproof dish. Melt the butter, then add the olive oil and mix together. Brush the mixture over the potatoes, then season well with salt and pepper. Sprinkle over the breadcrumbs and cheese.

3 Roast the potatoes in the oven for about 1 hour, depending on their size, until golden brown and fanned apart along the cut lines. Serve hot.

This dish is named after the Stockholm restaurant that created it, and is a method of cooking rather than a recipe. Choose similar-sized potatoes so that they cook uniformly, and the essential thing is to cut the potatoes most of the way, but not completely, through.

Grated Potato Casserole Riivinkropsu

Serves 4

a small knob (pat) of butter
2 eggs
250ml/8fl oz/1 cup full-fat (whole)
  milk
30ml/2 tbsp plain (all-purpose) flour
5ml/1 tsp salt
2 potatoes
15ml/1 tbsp chopped fresh parsley,
  to garnish (optional)

*This recipe comes from
Satakunta, a south-western
region of Finland. Floury,
maincrop potatoes will
produce the best results.*

1 Preheat the oven to 180°C/350°F/Gas 4. Grease an ovenproof dish with the butter. Beat the eggs together in a bowl then add the milk and mix together. Add the flour and salt and mix to form a batter.

2 Peel the potatoes, then grate them and add to the batter. Transfer the potato mixture to the prepared dish, then bake in the oven for about 50 minutes, until the potatoes are cooked. Serve hot, sprinkled with chopped parsley, if using.

VARIATION

To make a richer, creamier version, substitute half the milk with single (light) cream.

Sauerkraut Pie Hapankaalipiiras

1 To make the pastry, put the flour and salt in a large bowl. Cut the butter into small pieces, add to the flour and rub in until the mixture resembles fine breadcrumbs. Alternatively, put the flour and salt in a food processor, add the butter and, using a pulsing action, blend to form fine breadcrumbs. Add the oil and water and mix to form a dough. Shape into a ball, cover with a clean dish towel, then leave to rest in the refrigerator for 1 hour.

2 Rinse the sauerkraut in cold running water if necessary, then put in a pan with the butter and sugar and heat for 1–2 minutes. Add the wine, cover the pan, bring the mixture to the boil, then remove from the heat.

3 Cook the shredded white and the Savoy cabbage in boiling salted water for about 5 minutes until tender, then drain, refresh under cold running water, and drain again. Put in a bowl and add the sauerkraut and ham. Mix together well and transfer to a deep, ovenproof pie dish.

4 Preheat the oven to 180°C/350°F/Gas 4. Roll out the pastry on a lightly floured surface so that it is large enough to cover the dish, and place it over the dish. Combine the egg yolk and water and brush over the pie to glaze. Bake in the oven for 20 minutes or until the pastry is golden brown. Serve hot.

VARIATION

To make the dish more substantial, replace the ham with some meatballs.

Serves 4

300g/11oz sauerkraut
20g/¾oz/1½ tbsp butter
5ml/1 tsp sugar
100ml/3½fl oz/scant ½ cup white
    wine
150g/5oz white cabbage, shredded
150g/5oz Savoy cabbage, shredded
150g/5oz boiled ham, cubed
1 egg yolk
5ml/1 tsp water

For the pastry

275g/10oz/2½ cups plain
    (all-purpose) flour
5ml/1 tsp salt
150g/5oz/10 tbsp unsalted butter
45ml/3 tbsp vegetable oil
25ml/1½ tbsp water

Traditionally made with a thin crust of yeast or puff pastry, this delicious pie can be eaten on its own or as an accompaniment to roasted meat. This version uses shortcrust pastry, and is filled with a mixture of sauerkraut, two types of cabbage and chunks of ham.

Beetroot Patties
Punajuuripihvit

Serves 4

2 cooked beetroots (beets)
1 egg, beaten
100g/3¾oz/2 cups fine fresh
    breadcrumbs
vegetable oil, for shallow frying
salt and ground black pepper
sour cream, to serve

In the days before air-freighted vegetables, beetroot was a staple ingredient in Finland, and was the basis for a wide variety of imaginative recipes. These delicious patties can be served with a dollop of sour cream as an appetizer or alongside grilled meat or fish to provide a different texture and flavour.

1 Peel the outer skin from the cooked beetroot using a sharp knife, then cut the flesh into 1cm/½in slices.

2 Break the egg on a plate and beat lightly. Spread the breadcrumbs on a separate plate and season with salt and pepper. Dip the beetroot slices in the egg and then the breadcrumbs, to coat both sides.

3 Heat the oil in a large frying pan, add the coated beetroot and fry for about 5 minutes, turning once, until golden brown on both sides. Drain on kitchen paper and serve hot, with sour cream.

Finnish Cucumber Salad in Sweet-and-sour Dressing Kurkkusalaatti

Serves 4

2 cucumbers
15ml/1 tbsp salt
30ml/2 tbsp white wine vinegar
30ml/2 tbsp caster (superfine) sugar
5ml/1 tsp ground black pepper
sour cream, to serve

This cucumber salad is made in two parts. First, the cucumber is salted and pressed to extract its juices and then it is squeezed to produce a different textured salad, which is dressed in a sweet-and-sour sugar and vinegar mixture. With a dollop of sour cream it makes a refreshing appetizer, and as a side dish it will cut through any fattiness or richness in stews or braised dishes.

1 Peel and thinly slice the cucumber. Place in a large bowl and sprinkle with the salt. Place a smaller bowl on top and add a heavy weight, such as a can or a full jam jar. Leave to press for 1 hour.

2 Mix the vinegar, sugar and pepper in a bowl. Taste to check that the balance of sharpness to sweetness is good and adjust if necessary.

3 Lift out the salted cucumber, a handful at a time, and squeeze out as much liquid and salt as possible. Toss in the vinegar and sugar mixture and transfer to a serving dish. Serve with a spoonful of sour cream.

COOK'S TIP

Cucumber loses volume when it is prepared in this way, so allow at least half a cucumber per person.

Smoked Fish Salad Savutettu kalasalaatti

Serves 4

500g/1¼lb smoked eel fillet
5ml/1 tsp Swedish or German
    mustard
5ml/1 tsp grated fresh horseradish
about 50ml/2fl oz/¼ cup double
    (heavy) cream
4 smoked sprats, skinned and filleted
ground black pepper
lettuce and boiled new potatoes,
    to serve

For the dressing

100ml/3½fl oz/scant ½ cup double
    (heavy) cream
5ml/1 tsp mustard
5ml/1 tsp grated fresh horseradish
a little lemon juice

1 Remove the skin from the smoked eel by peeling it off with your fingers, much as you would skin a banana. Place the skinned, smoked eel on a board and cut about half of it into four neat fillets. Set aside.

2 Put the remaining smoked eel fillet in a food processor, add the mustard and horseradish and season with pepper. Blend until smooth, adding enough cream to form a firm paste.

3 Spoon a dollop of the smoked eel paste or pâté on to a bed of lettuce on four individual serving plates.

4 Carefully remove the skin from the smoked sprats using a small, sharp knife, then arrange the skinned fish around the pâté, together with the reserved smoked eel fillets.

5 To make the dressing, whisk together the cream, mustard, horseradish and a few drops of lemon juice, until stiff. Spoon on to the salad and serve with boiled new potatoes.

COOK'S TIP

The root of fresh horseradish resembles a knobbly parsnip. It is very versatile, and lends a pungent flavour to vegetable, meat and fish dishes, as well as making an excellent condiment.

Oily fish – such as salmon, eels, sprats, perch, trout and herring – are delicious when smoked. The fish used in this recipe are hot-smoked, a process that involves cooking and smoking the fish simultaneously over chips of burning wood (such as alder, apple or juniper) or, more recently, in an electric kiln. The smokiness and rich, oily flesh of the cooked fish is particularly suited to sharp dressings, such as this simple yet delicious horseradish and mustard one.

Salmon Bake Lohipaistos

1 To make the Pressed Salmon and Dill, put the salt, sugar, dill, brandy and pepper in a bowl and mix together. Rub the mixture over both sides of the salmon fillets. Place the flesh sides of the fillets together, so that the skin sides are on the outside to form a whole fish, and wrap in foil.

2 Place the wrapped fish in a deep dish or roasting pan and place a heavy weight or weights, such as cans, on the top. Put in the refrigerator and leave for 12 hours. Turn the fish over, replace the weights and leave for a further 12 hours. Scrape off the marinade and pat the fish dry with kitchen paper.

3 To prepare the Salmon Bake, preheat the oven to 200°C/400°F/ Gas 6. Grease a deep, ovenproof dish with a little of the butter.

4 Arrange half the potato slices in a layer over the base of the dish, then add a layer of salmon and a layer of onion. Sprinkle over the dill and end with a layer of the remaining potato slices.

5 Mix the eggs, milk, salt and pepper together and pour over the dish. Dot the remaining butter on top. Bake in the oven for 1 hour, until the potatoes are tender. Serve immediately.

Serves 4

25g/1oz/2 tbsp unsalted
　butter, softened
8 potatoes, thinly sliced
300g/11oz Pressed Salmon with Dill,
　sliced (see below)
1 onion, finely chopped
30ml/2 tbsp chopped fresh dill
3 eggs, beaten
400ml/14fl oz/1⅔ cups milk
5ml/1 tsp salt
2.5ml/½ tsp ground white pepper

**For the Pressed Salmon with Dill
　(Graavilohi)**

90ml/6 tbsp coarse sea salt
90ml/6 tbsp sugar
90ml/6 tbsp chopped fresh dill
30ml/2 tbsp brandy
5ml/1 tsp ground black pepper
1 small or ½ large fresh salmon,
　filleted

Subtly flavoured with dill and onion, this warming bake combines two of the most common ingredients in Finland: salmon and potatoes. The recipe calls for graavilohi – salmon that has been pressed with salt, dill and brandy for 24 hours – which can be used in a number of recipes, or thinly sliced and simply served with a dill and crème fraîche sauce.

Trout with Cucumber and Horseradish
Taimen kurkun ja piparjuuren kanssa

Serves 4

1 cucumber, thinly sliced
75g/3oz/6 tbsp butter, softened,
  plus extra for greasing
5ml/1 tsp Dijon mustard
20g/¾oz grated horseradish
a few drops of lemon juice
600g/1lb 6oz trout fillet, cut into
  twelve 50g/2oz thin slices
45ml/3 tbsp water or white wine
salt and ground black pepper

1 Sprinkle the cucumber slices with 2.5ml/½ tsp salt and mix together. Sandwich the slices between two plates, place a small weight on top and leave in the refrigerator for 30 minutes. Squeeze out any juices from the cucumber.

2 Preheat the oven to 200°C/400°F/Gas 6. Grease a shallow, ovenproof dish with butter and sprinkle a little salt over the base. Put the softened butter in a bowl and beat until it is light and fluffy, then add the mustard, horseradish, lemon juice and a little pepper, and beat until well mixed.

3 Arrange the trout slices in the prepared dish in four servings, each consisting of three overlapping slices. Spread these with the horseradish butter. Arrange the cucumber slices across the top of each serving, to look like fish scales.

4 Add water or white wine to the dish, then cover with foil. Bake in the oven for 6–7 minutes until just tender. Using a fish slice, carefully transfer each serving to a warmed plate and serve hot.

COOK'S TIP

It is very easy to overcook trout, which makes it dry. You need to remember that residual heat on the outside of the fish will continue to cook the centre for as long as it remains warm, so it should be served as soon as it is ready.

Horseradish is one of the principal aromatics in Finnish cooking. Used with care, it gives zest to a dish rather than overpowers it. If you are able to use fresh horseradish and grate it yourself, so much the better.

Fried Sprats in Rye Flour
Silakkapihvit

1 To make the Tartare Sauce, whisk the egg yolks, mustard and vinegar in a bowl. Slowly add the oil, drop by drop at first, then, when it begins to thicken, in a slow, steady stream, whisking all the time until the sauce begins to thicken like mayonnaise. Stir in the anchovy essence, chopped gherkin, capers and parsley into the sauce and season to taste with salt and pepper. Store in the refrigerator until ready to use.

2 To prepare the sprats, cut off the head and tail, make a slit along the belly and remove the guts. Cut the backbone near the head and remove the backbone. Open the fish out like a book. Season the insides of the fish with salt and pepper and sprinkle over the chopped chives. Place two fish together so that the flesh sides are pressed against one another and the skin sides are on the outside.

3 Break the egg on to a plate and beat together with the milk. Spread the rye flour and the breadcrumbs on separate plates. Dip the pairs of fish in the rye flour, to coat on both sides, then in the beaten egg and finally the breadcrumbs.

4 Heat the oil in a large frying pan, add the coated fish and fry for about 5 minutes on each side until crisp and tender. Serve whilst still hot, with the Tartare Sauce.

Serves 4

8 sprats
60ml/4 tbsp chopped fresh chives
1 egg
45ml/3 tbsp milk
50g/2oz/½ cup rye flour
200g/7oz/4 cups fine fresh
    breadcrumbs
vegetable oil, for shallow frying
salt and ground white pepper

For the Tartare Sauce

2 egg yolks
15ml/1 tbsp Swedish or German
    mustard
15ml/1 tbsp white wine vinegar
200ml/7fl oz/scant 1 cup vegetable
    oil
5ml/1 tsp anchovy essence (paste)
15ml/1 tbsp chopped gherkin
15ml/1 tbsp chopped capers
15ml/1 tbsp chopped fresh parsley
salt and ground black pepper

Home-made tartare sauce can be a little time-consuming, but the results are definitely worth it. Baltic sprats have soft bones, like sardines, so they can be eaten without discomfort if you don't want to pick them out.

Serves 4

1kg/2¼lb burbot or monkfish, with
their bones, if filleted
20g/¾oz/1½ tbsp unsalted butter
1 onion, chopped
1 small celery stick, chopped
1 small leek, chopped
1 bay leaf
10 whole allspice
5 white peppercorns
15ml/1 tbsp salt
1.5 litres/2½ pints/6¼ cups water
1 carrot, finely diced
500g/1¼lb potatoes, cubed
5ml/1 tsp plain white (all-purpose)
flour
200ml/7fl oz/scant 1 cup double
(heavy) cream
salt and ground white pepper
dill sprigs, to garnish

Burbot Chowder Madekeitto

1 Fillet the fish or, if the fishmonger fillets it for you, ask him or her to reserve the bones and head. Cut the fish into large chunks.

2 Heat the butter in a pan, add the chopped onion, celery, leek, fish bones, fish head and any fish trimmings. Fry for about 5 minutes until the vegetables are beginning to soften. Add the bay leaf, allspice, peppercorns, 15ml/1 tbsp salt and 1 litre/1¾ pints/4 cups of the water. Bring to the boil, then lower the heat and simmer gently for 30 minutes.

3 Strain the stock through a sieve (strainer) into a clean pan. (You should be left with about 1 litre/1¾ pints/4 cups of liquid. If you do not have enough, add extra water to make up the correct amount.)

4 Add the carrot and potato to the stock and bring to the boil. Lower the heat and simmer until the potato is nearly cooked. The timing will vary depending upon the size of the potato cubes and the variety of the potato.

5 Add the fish to the pan and return to simmering point, then sprinkle over the flour and continue to simmer for a further 5 minutes, or until the fish is just cooked.

6 Stir in the cream, then taste and add salt and pepper according to taste. Pour into individual serving dishes and serve hot, garnished with a sprig of dill.

Burbot is a large freshwater fish that looks similar to a monkfish, and which has soft but well-flavoured flesh. In fact, years ago, their similarity led to both fish being called burbot. This hearty chowder can be served on its own as a tasty appetizer or with bread for a sustaining main meal.

Elk and Celeriac Casserole Hirvipata

1 Preheat the oven to 180°C/350°F/Gas 4. Cut the elk meat into chunky cubes, then season with salt and pepper.

2 Heat the oil in a flameproof and ovenproof dish, then add the meat, chopped onions and carrots. Fry the meat and vegetables until the vegetables soften and the meat is brown on all sides.

3 Add the water, celeriac and juniper berries to the pan, bring to the boil then cover. Cook in the oven for 2 hours, or until the meat is tender.

4 Remove the casserole from the oven and dust the surface of the liquid with the flour, and stir to combine with and thicken the sauce. Return the dish to the oven and cook for a further 10 minutes.

5 Stir in the blackcurrant jelly and the wine vinegar. If necessary, adjust the consistency by adding a little more water. Taste and add salt and pepper if needed.

6 Finally, stir in the butter until it has melted and is completely incorporated. Serve the casserole immediately.

COOK'S TIP
The addition of the butter improves the texture of the cooking liquid and adds a touch of creaminess to the dense meat.

Elks are large animals, cousins of the North American moose, just as reindeer are related to caribou. The meat is dark and tastes similar to venison, which can be used as a good substitute if you are unable to buy elk meat. Serve this rich, warming stew on its own or, for a more sustaining meal, with creamy mashed potatoes or lightly boiled new potatoes, and some steamed green vegetables.

Serves 4

1kg/2¼lb boneless elk, preferably
  from the hindquarter
30ml/2 tbsp vegetable oil
2 onions, roughly chopped
2 carrots, roughly chopped
750ml/1¼ pints/3 cups water
1 small celeriac, cubed
8 juniper berries
30ml/2 tbsp plain (all-purpose) flour
15ml/1 tbsp blackcurrant jelly
15ml/1 tbsp wine vinegar
25g/1oz/2 tbsp unsalted butter
salt and ground black pepper

Reindeer Fillet with Morel Mushrooms
Poro sienikastikkeessa

Serves 4

25g/1oz dried morel mushrooms
100ml/3½fl oz/scant ½ cup plus
   15ml/1 tbsp water
1 shallot, finely chopped
5ml/1 tsp potato flour
45ml/3 tbsp crème fraîche
1 gherkin, thinly sliced lengthways
4 boneless steaks cut from saddles
   of reindeer (caribou) or another
   type of venison, about 200g/7oz
   each
vegetable oil, for grilling or frying
25g/1oz/2 tbsp unsalted butter
salt and ground black pepper

1 Put the morels in a pan, add the 100ml/3½fl oz/scant ½ cup water and bring to the boil. Remove from the heat and leave to cool. Once cool, strain the liquid into a clean pan, reserving the morels. Add the shallot to the pan.

2 Put the potato flour in a bowl, add the 15ml/1 tbsp water and blend together. Add the mixture to the pan and bring to the boil, stirring all the time, until slightly thickened. Carefully strain the sauce into a clean pan, then add the reserved morels, crème fraîche and gherkin.

3 Brush the reindeer or other venison steaks with oil, then season with salt and pepper. Grill (broil) or fry the steaks for about 5 minutes, depending on how rare you like your meat.

4 Whisk any cooking juices from the steaks into the sauce along with the unsalted butter and reheat gently. Serve the steaks, accompanied by the morel sauce.

COOK'S TIP

Morel mushrooms, even dried ones, can be gritty, so leave the cooking liquid a few minutes after straining them so that any grit sinks to the bottom. Strain most of the liquid into a clean pan, leaving the grit behind in the liquid that remains.

Reindeer, like elk, should not be overcooked or the meat can become tough. Here, the fillet is pan-fried and served with a creamy morel mushroom sauce. Morel mushrooms grow in early summer, ahead of the main fungi season. Often sold in their dried form, they lend a distinct and individual flavour to any dish.

Beef and Mushroom Meatloaf
Sieni-ja lihamureke

1 Preheat the oven to 200°C/400°F/Gas 6. Grease a 450g/1lb loaf tin (pan) or small, deep ovenproof dish.

2 Put the mushrooms in a bowl. Add the breadcrumbs and cream and mix together. Add the minced beef, onion, egg, rosemary, salt and pepper and knead the ingredients together into a ball.

3 Transfer the mixture to the prepared tin or dish, cover with foil and bake in the oven for 40 minutes, until it feels firm when pressed with an upturned fork or spoon.

4 Meanwhile, make the creamed mushrooms. In a medium pan, boil the button mushrooms in the double cream for 5 minutes, or until the mushrooms are tender. Season to taste with salt, ground black pepper and grated nutmeg.

5 Turn out the meatloaf and serve hot, with creamed mushrooms and a tossed salad.

Serves 4

150g/5oz mushrooms, finely
   chopped
50g/2oz/1 cup fine fresh
   breadcrumbs
100ml/3½fl oz/scant ½ cup double
   (heavy) cream
250g/9oz minced (ground) beef
1 onion, chopped
1 egg, beaten
5ml/1 tsp chopped rosemary leaves
5ml/1 tsp salt
1.5ml/¼ tsp ground white pepper
15g/½oz/1 tbsp butter, for greasing
tossed salad, to serve

For the creamed mushrooms

200g/7oz sliced mushrooms
100ml/3½fl oz/scant ½ cup double
   (heavy) cream
salt and ground black pepper
pinch of nutmeg

Ideally, this moreish dish will include woodland mushrooms, such as cep or girolle, but cultivated mushrooms are also very good. Use flat rather than button mushrooms, as they have more flavour. The same mixture can also be formed into patties and fried in a little butter.

Liver, Rice and Treacle Pudding Maksalaatikko

1 Bring the water and salt to the boil in a pan that has a lid. Add the rice then, stirring continuously to prevent sticking, boil until the water evaporates. Add the milk, lower the heat, cover, and simmer for about 30 minutes until cooked through.

2 Preheat the oven to 180°C/350°F/Gas 4. Grease a shallow ovenproof dish with butter. Melt the remaining butter in a pan, add the onion and fry for 5 minutes, until softened but not browned. Stir the onion into the cooked rice.

3 Put the liver in the bowl of a food processor and chop until fine but not puréed. Alternatively, finely chop by hand. Transfer to a bowl. Add the eggs, treacle, raisins, marjoram and pepper to the chopped liver and whisk together. Combine with the cooked rice.

4 Pour the mixture into the dish and bake in the oven for 1 hour 10 minutes to 1 hour 15 minutes, until the mixture is firm when you press it with an upturned fork. Serve hot, garnished with lingonberries or another sharp berry.

COOK'S TIP

The choice of liver will affect the final flavour but you can use most varieties, except for poultry livers, which are too delicate to compete with the other flavours.

Serves 4

200ml/7fl oz/scant 1 cup water
15ml/1 tbsp salt
150g/5oz/¾ cup short grain rice
1 litre/1¾ pints/4 cups milk
25g/1oz/2 tbsp butter, plus extra
    for greasing
1 onion, finely chopped
400g/14oz calf's, lamb's or pig's
    liver
2 eggs
60ml/4 tbsp treacle (molasses) or
    dark corn syrup
100g/3¾oz/⅔ cup raisins
2.5ml/½ tsp dried marjoram
2.5ml/½ tsp ground white pepper
lingonberries or another sharp berry,
    such as cranberries, to garnish

This combination of ingredients may seem eccentric, but it tastes magnificent. The astringency of the liver is balanced by the sweetness of the dark syrup and raisins, and the finished dish is balanced by sharp lingonberries.

Wild Duck with Parsnips and Sauerkraut Gravy
Sorsaa ja palsternakkaa hapankaalikastikkeessa

Serves 2–4

2 mallards
50g/2oz/¼ cup goose fat
1 onion, chopped
1 small celery stick, chopped
300ml/10fl oz/1¼ cups beer
2kg/4½lb parsnips
25g/2oz/2 tbsp butter
15ml/1 tbsp milk
100g/3¾oz sauerkraut
5ml/1 tsp treacle (molasses)
salt and ground black pepper

Hunted during the autumn and winter, wild duck come in several guises. This recipe uses mallard, one of which will provide a generous serving or two smaller servings. Served with both mashed and roasted parsnips and a thick sauerkraut gravy, this delectable dish makes an ideal meal on a cold night.

1 Preheat the oven to 200°C/400°F/Gas 6. To prepare the ducks, cut the legs away from the carcasses. Also cut away the wishbone. Season the duck legs with salt and pepper. Set aside the breast portions.

2 Heat a third of the goose fat in a flameproof casserole, add the duck legs and fry until browned on all sides. Add the onion and celery and then the beer. Cover and cook in the oven for at least 1 hour, until tender.

3 Meanwhile, prepare the parsnips; divide the parsnips into broad bases and thinner stems. Heat half the remaining goose fat in a roasting pan, add the thinner stems and roast in the oven for about 20 minutes or until crisp.

4 Dice the parsnip bases and put in a pan of water. Bring to the boil, then reduce the heat and simmer for about 20 minutes, until tender. Drain the parsnips, return to the pan and mash until smooth. Beat in the butter and milk, then season. Set aside and keep warm.

5 Heat the remaining goose fat in a large frying pan, add the reserved duck breast portions, still on the bone, and sear on both sides. Transfer to a separate roasting pan and roast for 15 minutes. Carve the breast portions away from the bone.

6 To prepare the gravy, skim any excess fat from the pan in which the duck legs have been cooked. Strain the remaining juices into the pan used to cook the duck breast portions. On top of the stove, bring the mixture to the boil, stirring to deglaze the pan and incorporate any sediment from the pan. Add the sauerkraut and treacle and stir together.

7 To serve, slice the breast portions lengthways into thin strips. Place a scoop of mashed parsnip in the middle of warmed serving plates, lay the sliced breast meat across the top, add a roasted duck leg, some roast parsnips and pour over the sauerkraut gravy.

Serves 4

150ml/5fl oz/⅔ cup water
50g/2oz/¼ cup short grain rice
500ml/17fl oz/generous 2 cups milk
butter, for greasing
2 large eggs
50g/2oz/¼ cup caster (superfine)
    sugar
90g/3½oz/¾ cup plain (all-purpose)
    flour
2.5ml/½ tsp salt
strawberry, raspberry or cloudberry
    jam or fresh seasonal berries, to
    serve

COOK'S TIPS

• Short grain rice has a high starch content, which makes the grains sticky when cooked.
• To make this dish even more creamy, pour some double (heavy) cream over the hot dessert once you have spooned it into bowls.

Åland Island Pancake
Ahvenanmaan pannukakku

1 Put the water and rice in a pan, bring to the boil, then reduce the heat and simmer, stirring occasionally to prevent the rice from sticking, for about 30 minutes, until all the water is absorbed.

2 Add 150ml/¼ pint/⅔ cup of the milk to the pan and simmer until all the liquid has been absorbed. (The rice will still be quite hard.)

3 Preheat the oven to 180°C/350°F/Gas 4. Generously grease a deep, ovenproof dish with butter.

4 Meanwhile, put the eggs, sugar, flour, salt and the remaining 350ml/ 12fl oz/1½ cups of milk in a large bowl and beat together to form a slack batter. Stir in the partially cooked rice.

5 Pour the mixture into the prepared dish and bake in the oven for 30 minutes, until the mixture is set and the top has turned a golden colour.

6 Spoon the dessert into individual serving bowls and serve hot, with jam, or fresh berries when they are in season.

The Åland islands lie in the Baltic Sea between Sweden and Finland. Like much of western Finland, the islanders are Swedish speaking, and have a distinctive cooking heritage that reflects their varied history of rule by Danes, Swedes, Russians and Finns. For this dessert, think of a batter or rice pudding rather than the thin wafers we normally associate with the word pancake. Serve warm with jam or fresh berries when they are in season.

Beestings Pudding Uunijuusto

Serves 4

20g/¾oz/1½ tbsp butter
2.5ml/½ tsp salt
1 litre/1¾ pints/4 cups beestings

To serve

caster (superfine) sugar
ground cinnamon

1 Preheat the oven to 200°C/400°F/Gas 6. Grease a 1.5 litre/2½ pint deep, ovenproof dish with the butter. Mix the salt with the beestings, then pour into the prepared dish.

2 Bake in the oven for 35–40 minutes, until set. Serve hot, cut into slices and dusted with sugar and cinnamon.

Beestings is an age-old ingredient, still easily obtained in cattle and dairy farming regions around the world. It is the first milk produced by a cow after calving and is thicker, richer and creamier than ordinary milk.

Bilberry Tart Mustikkapiirakka

Makes 1 medium tart
600g/1lb 6oz bilberries
15ml/1 tbsp potato flour
50g/2oz/¼ cup caster (superfine)
   sugar

For the pastry
150g/5oz/10 tbsp unsalted butter
1 egg
50ml/2fl oz/¼ cup double (heavy)
   cream
125g/4¼oz/generous ½ cup plain
   (all-purpose) flour

1 To make the pastry, put the butter in a large bowl and beat until creamy. Add the egg and cream and mix together, then add the flour and mix to form a dough. Cover and leave to rest in the refrigerator for 3–4 hours or, preferably, overnight.

2 Preheat the oven to 200°C/400°F/Gas 6. Put the bilberries, potato flour and sugar in a bowl and mix together.

3 On a lightly floured surface, roll out the pastry to a 30cm/12in round, 1cm/½in thick. Place on a baking sheet and spoon the bilberry mixture on top, leaving a border around the edges. Bake in the oven for about 30 minutes until the pastry is cooked through.

COOK'S TIP
The function of the potato flour is to soak up excess juice from the berries as they cook. If preferred, substitute 30ml/2 tbsp ground biscuits.

Bilberries are wild blueberries. They are a seasonal fruit and are not always available, so use the cultivated ones if necessary. The rich, crumbly pastry is made with cream as well as butter, which makes it quite soft to handle, so be sure to rest it well before rolling out and baking.

Cloudberry Mousse Lakkavanukas

Serves 4

60ml/4 tbsp cold water
4 gelatine sheets
60ml/4 tbsp hot water
100g/3¾oz/generous ⅓ cup
   cloudberry jam
45ml/3 tbsp Lakka (Finnish
   cloudberry liqueur)
100g/3¾oz cloudberries or
   cloudberry jam
100g/3¾oz/scant 1 cup cream
   cheese
200ml/7fl oz/scant 1 cup double
   (heavy) cream
30ml/2 tbsp sugar
seeds from 1 vanilla pod (bean)
15ml/1 tbsp lemon juice

1 Put 30ml/2 tbsp of the cold water in a bowl, add two gelatine sheets and leave to soak for 5 minutes. Squeeze the sheets into a bowl, add 30ml/2 tbsp of the hot water and stir until dissolved.

2 Put the cloudberry jam and liqueur in a bowl and mix to combine, then mix in the dissolved gelatine. Stir in the berries or the jam.

3 Beat the cream cheese in a large bowl. Pour the double cream into a separate bowl and whisk until it holds its shape. Fold into the cream cheese with the sugar, vanilla seeds and lemon juice.

4 Soak the remaining two gelatine sheets in the remaining 30ml/2 tbsp cold water. Squeeze the sheets into a bowl, add the remaining 30ml/ 2 tbsp of the hot water and stir until dissolved. Stir the dissolved gelatine into the cream mixture.

5 Put both the mixtures in the refrigerator for an hour or until setting point is reached. Meanwhile, line four large ramekin dishes with clear film (plastic wrap).

6 Just before the mixtures sets, spoon alternate layers of each mixture into the prepared ramekin dishes. Return to the refrigerator and leave to set. To serve, turn out of the dishes on to individual serving plates.

*The Arctic cloudberry is a close relative of the raspberry.
They are golden-yellow in colour and grow naturally in the
high northern hemisphere – Finland, Russia and Canada.
As well as eating them raw and in jams, Finns make a
sweet liqueur called Lakka from the berries, which can
also be used to sweeten recipes.*

Almond Biscuits Manteliässät

Makes 20

200g/7oz/1 cup caster (superfine) sugar
150g/5oz/10 tbsp butter
3 eggs
100g/3¾oz/scant 1 cup ground almonds
350g/12oz/3 cups plain (all-purpose) flour

To decorate

caster (superfine) sugar
nibbed (chopped) almonds

1 Preheat the oven to 180°C/350°F/Gas 4. Put the sugar and butter in a large bowl and beat together until light and fluffy. Add the eggs, one at a time, beating well after each addition, then add the almonds and flour. Mix together to make a dough, then form into a ball.

2 On a lightly floured surface, roll out the dough quite thinly and cut into finger-thick strips. Cut the strips into 4cm/1½in lengths and twist each piece into an S shape.

3 Place the strips on a baking tray and sprinkle with caster sugar and nibbed almonds. Bake in the oven for about 10 minutes, or until just golden brown.

These little almond biscuits can be served as part of a selection with coffee or as an accompaniment to a creamy dessert.

Raspberry Jam Biscuits Vadelmapyörykät

Serves 4

100g/3¾oz/generous ½ cup caster (superfine) sugar

100g/3¾oz/scant ½ cup unsalted butter

1 egg

100ml/3½fl oz/scant ½ cup sour cream

350g/12oz/3 cups plain (all-purpose) flour

5ml/1 tsp baking powder (baking soda)

90ml/6 tbsp raspberry jam

These simple biscuits are given an extra dimension by the addition of sour cream. Make plenty, as they will be popular with all the family.

1 Preheat the oven to 180°C/350°F/Gas 4. Put the sugar and butter in a large bowl and beat together until light and fluffy. Beat in the egg, then mix in the sour cream. Sift the flour and baking powder together, then incorporate into the mixture, which will have a fairly wet consistency.

2 On a lightly floured surface, roll out the dough to 5mm/¼in thickness then, using a floured 5cm/2in round cutter, cut out rounds and place on a baking tray. Leave to rest for 15 minutes.

3 Press the centre of each round with your thumb or the back of a teaspoon, then spoon a little raspberry jam into the indentation. Bake in the oven for about 12–15 minutes, until golden. Leave to cool on a wire rack.

Coffee Bread Pulla

1 Melt 115g/4oz/½ cup of the butter and leave to cool. Crush the cardamom pods with a pestle and mortar to yield about 5ml/1 tsp powder. Put the dried or fresh yeast in a large bowl, add the water and stir until dissolved. Stir in the milk, sugar, salt, eggs and cardamom.

2 Stir in one-quarter of the flour to form a batter, then beat until smooth. Add a further one-quarter of the flour and the melted butter and stir well, then beat until the dough is shiny. Stir the remaining flour into the dough, then turn on to a floured surface and knead until the dough feels smooth and elastic. Cover the dough and leave to rest for 15 minutes.

3 Knead the dough again until it is shiny, then put in a bowl, cover and leave in a warm place to rise for at least an hour, or until doubled in size.Repeat the process by knocking back the dough, kneading well and leaving once more to rise for about an hour or until doubled in size.

4 Grease three baking sheets with butter. Turn the dough out on to a lightly floured work surface and cut into three equal-sized pieces, then cut each of these into three equal-sized pieces.

5 Shape each piece of dough into a ball, then roll into 40cm/16in long strips. Pinch the ends of three strips together, then braid them and pinch the ends to seal. Repeat with the remaining pieces of dough to make three loaves. Place on the baking sheets and leave to rise in a warm place for about an hour or until puffy.

6 Preheat the oven to 200ºC/400ºF/Gas 6. Brush the loaves with beaten egg to glaze and sprinkle with sugar and almonds. Bake in the oven for 25 minutes until golden brown. Serve warm, cut into slices.

Pulla is the universal accompaniment to coffee in Finland.
It is a sweet bread, with a cardamom-scented flavour,
and is traditionally braided.

Makes 3 loaves

115g/4oz/½ cup butter, plus extra
  for greasing
10 cardamom pods, seeded
1 packet easy-blend (rapid-rise) dried
  yeast or 25g/1oz fresh yeast
120ml/4fl oz/½ cup lukewarm water
475ml/16fl oz/2 cups milk
200g/7oz/1 cup caster (superfine)
  sugar
5ml/1 tsp salt
4 eggs, beaten
900g/2lb/8 cups plain (all-purpose)
  flour
beaten egg, to glaze
sugar and nibbed (chopped) almonds,
  to decorate

COOK'S TIP

These loaves freeze well. To serve, simply defrost completely and then warm in the oven for about 10 minutes before serving.

Spice Cake Pehmeä maustekakku

Makes 1 cake

225g/8oz butter, plus extra for
    greasing
4 eggs
225g/8oz/generous 1 cup caster
    (superfine) sugar
5ml/1 tsp ground cardamom
5ml/1 tsp ground cinnamon
5ml/1 tsp ground ginger
15ml/1 tbsp grated orange rind
2.5ml/½ tsp bicarbonate of soda
    (baking soda)
300ml/10 fl oz/1¼ cups sour cream
225g/8oz/2 cups plain (all-purpose)
    flour

1 Preheat the oven to 200°C/400°F/Gas 6. Grease a 23cm/9in loose-bottomed cake tin (pan) or a standard-size kugelhopf mould with butter. Melt the remaining butter.

2 Put the eggs, sugar and butter in a bowl and whisk together until light and fluffy. Add the cardamom, cinnamon, ginger and grated orange rind and stir together.

3 Mix the bicarbonate of soda into the sour cream, then add to the egg mixture. Finally, add the flour and mix together.

4 Pour the mixture into the prepared tin and bake in the oven for 1 hour, until brown and a skewer inserted in the middle comes out clean. Leave to cool in the tin, or remove from the tin and cool on a wire rack.

COOK'S TIPS
• Single (light) cream can be substituted for the sour cream but you should then replace the bicarbonate of soda (baking soda) with 5ml/1 tsp baking powder.
• If you have a kugelhopf mould then this can be used to give the finished cake a more interesting shape and greater presence.

Finnish home-baking tends to be quite simple and does not often include fancy ingredients. The addition of various spices, however, elevates the cakes and bakes, producing delicious and aromatic results.

Christmas Stars Joulutähdet

Makes 10

200g/7oz/generous ½ cups plain (all-purpose) flour
5ml/1 tsp baking powder (baking soda)
125g/4½oz/9 tbsp butter, softened
150ml/5fl oz/⅔ cup cold water, or enough to bind
200g/7oz/scant 1 cup ready-to-eat prunes
1 egg, beaten, to glaze

COOK'S TIP

A little brandy, mixed into the prunes, adds an extra dimension.

1 Preheat the oven to 200°C/400°F/Gas 6. Sift the flour and baking powder into a large bowl. Cut the butter into small pieces, add to the flour and rub in until the mixture resembles fine breadcrumbs. Alternatively, put the flour and baking powder in a food processor, add the butter and, using a pulsating action, blend to form fine breadcrumbs. Gradually add cold water and mix until it forms a dough.

2 On a lightly floured surface, roll out the pastry to a square 3mm/⅛in thick, then cut into ten squares. Make a diagonal cut from each corner of the squares towards the centre.

3 Chop the prunes into small pieces. Put a spoonful of chopped prunes in the centre of each square of pastry, then lift each corner of the pastry and fold it over to the centre to form a star.

4 Place the stars on a baking sheet and brush with beaten egg. Bake in the oven for 15 minutes, until golden brown. Cool on a wire rack.

These pretty pastries are Finland's answer to mince pies, although the prune filling is less sweet than mincemeat and does not include any alcohol.

Runeberg's Cakes Runebergin leivokset

Makes 12

175g/6oz/1½ cups plain
    (all-purpose) flour
5ml/1 tsp baking powder
2 eggs
150g/5oz/¾ cup caster (superfine)
    sugar
200g/7oz/scant 1 cup unsalted
    butter, plus extra for greasing
90g/3½oz/scant 1 cup ground
    almonds
125g/4¼oz/generous 2 cups fine
    fresh breadcrumbs
about 75ml/5 tbsp almond liqueur,
    such as Amaretto di Sarone
150g/5oz/½ cup raspberry jam

*These cakes appear
everywhere in February, to
celebrate the birthday of one
of Finland's most popular
poets, Johan Runeberg.
Although Swedish, Runeberg
spent his whole life in Finland
and he is regarded as a
national poet. They make a
delectable tea-time treat.*

1 Preheat the oven to 200°C/400°F/Gas 6. Grease twelve dariol or castle pudding tins (pans). Sift the flour and baking powder together into a bowl. Put the eggs and sugar in a large bowl and whisk together until light and fluffy.

2 In a separate bowl, beat the butter until creamy, then beat in the ground almonds and breadcrumbs. Add the mixture to the eggs and sugar and mix together, then stir in the sifted flour.

3 Divide the mixture between the prepared tins, allowing some room for the mixture to rise. Bake in the oven for 15–20 minutes, until a skewer inserted in the middle comes out clean. Leave to cool in the tins before turning out.

4 Brush the cakes with liqueur to dampen them, and then top each with a teaspoonful of raspberry jam.

Nutritional notes

Cep Mushroom Soup: Energy 262kcal/1081kJ; Protein 3.1g; Carbohydrate 7.8g, of which sugars 2.2g; Fat 24.5g, of which saturates 15g; Cholesterol 61mg; Calcium 46mg; Fibre 1.8g; Sodium 291mg.

Rustic Pea Soup with a Pig's Trotter: Energy 306kcal/1287kJ; Protein 26.8g; Carbohydrate 27.3g, of which sugars 2.8g; Fat 10.7g, of which saturates 3.6g; Cholesterol 42mg; Calcium 57mg; Fibre 5.7g; Sodium 869mg.

Hasselback Potatoes: Energy 380kcal/1593kJ; Protein 9.9g; Carbohydrate 42g, of which sugars 3.1g; Fat 20.4g, of which saturates 12.5g; Cholesterol 52mg; Calcium 182mg; Fibre 2.3g; Sodium 367mg.

Grated Potato Casserole: Energy 215kcal/894kJ; Protein 8.7g; Carbohydrate 13g, of which sugars 3.3g; Fat 14.7g, of which saturates 7.7g; Cholesterol 123mg; Calcium 277mg; Fibre 3g; Sodium 297mg.

Sauerkraut Pie: Energy 728kcal/3032kJ; Protein 16.3g; Carbohydrate 59.8g, of which sugars 7.4g; Fat 46.8g, of which saturates 24.1g; Cholesterol 163mg; Calcium 190mg; Fibre 5.4g; Sodium 1652mg.

Beetroot Patties: Energy 174kcal/734kJ; Protein 5.3g; Carbohydrate 23.2g, of which sugars 4.2g; Fat 7.4g, of which saturates 1g; Cholesterol 48mg; Calcium 50mg; Fibre 1.5g; Sodium 241mg.

Finnish Cucumber Salad in Sweet-and-sour Dressing: Energy 27kcal/114kJ; Protein 0.6g; Carbohydrate 6.4g, of which sugars 6.3g; Fat 0.1g, of which saturates 0g; Cholesterol 0mg; Calcium 16mg; Fibre 0.5g; Sodium 494mg.

Smoked Fish Salad: Energy 487kcal/2021kJ; Protein 30.8g; Carbohydrate 0.9g, of which sugars 0.7g; Fat 40.2g, of which saturates 17.3g; Cholesterol 285mg; Calcium 94mg; Fibre 0g; Sodium 257mg.

Salmon Bake: Energy 338kcal/1413kJ; Protein 24.3g; Carbohydrate 17.9g, of which sugars 10.2g; Fat 19.4g, of which saturates 7g; Cholesterol 199mg; Calcium 167mg; Fibre 0.7g; Sodium 665mg.

Trout with Cucumber and Horseradish: Energy 314kcal/1306kJ; Protein 29.7g; Carbohydrate 1g,

of which sugars 0.9g; Fat 21.3g, of which saturates 9.8g; Cholesterol 40mg; Calcium 27mg; Fibre 0.3g; Sodium 236mg.

Fried Sprats in Rye Flour: Energy 592kcal/2466kJ; Protein 18.8g; Carbohydrate 39.2g, of which sugars 1.7g; Fat 41g, of which saturates 5.7g; Cholesterol 156mg; Calcium 141mg; Fibre 1.3g; Sodium 601mg.

Burbot Chowder: Energy 582kcal/2431kJ; Protein 47.6g; Carbohydrate 25.8g, of which sugars 6.4g; Fat 32.6g, of which saturates 19.7g; Cholesterol 119mg; Calcium 77mg; Fibre 2.8g; Sodium 117mg.

Elk and Celeriac Casserole: Energy 452kcal/1901kJ; Protein 58g; Carbohydrate 20.8g, of which sugars 12.5g; Fat 17.4g, of which saturates 7.9g; Cholesterol 144mg; Calcium 83mg; Fibre 3.4g; Sodium 222mg.

Reindeer Fillet with Morel Mushrooms: Energy 357kcal/1495kJ; Protein 45.2g; Carbohydrate 2.8g, of which sugars 1.3g; Fat 19.6g, of which saturates 8.6g; Cholesterol 126mg; Calcium 25mg; Fibre 0.4g; Sodium 152mg.

Beef and Mushroom Meatloaf: Energy 366kcal/1517kJ; Protein 16.6g; Carbohydrate 11.5g, of which sugars 1.7g; Fat 28.5g, of which saturates 15.1g; Cholesterol 127mg; Calcium 48mg; Fibre 0.9g; Sodium 684mg.

Liver, Rice and Treacle Pudding: Energy 549kcal/2309kJ; Protein 33.6g; Carbohydrate 70.3g, of which sugars 40g; Fat 15.9g, of which saturates 7.7g; Cholesterol 493mg; Calcium 426mg; Fibre 0.7g; Sodium 294mg.

Wild Duck with Parsnips and Sauerkraut Gravy: Energy 657kcal/2756kJ; Protein 30.5g; Carbohydrate 66.8g, of which sugars 32.5g; Fat 29.9g, of which saturates 11.6g; Cholesterol 138mg; Calcium 254mg; Fibre 23.9g; Sodium 367mg.

Åland Island Pancake: Energy 265kcal/1121kJ; Protein 10.5g; Carbohydrate 46.4g, of which sugars 19.3g; Fat 5.3g, of which saturates 2.2g; Cholesterol 103mg; Calcium 205mg; Fibre 0.7g; Sodium 336mg.

Beestings Pudding: Energy 202kcal/838kJ; Protein 8.3g; Carbohydrate 11.3g, of which sugars 11.3g; Fat 13.9g, of which saturates 8.9g; Cholesterol 46mg; Calcium 296mg; Fibre 0g; Sodium 384mg.

Bilberry Tart: Energy 2266kcal/9452kJ; Protein 29.3g; Carbohydrate 190.7g, of which sugars 83.5g; Fat 159.2g, of which saturates 97.2g; Cholesterol 579mg; Calcium 435mg; Fibre 19.2g; Sodium 1016mg.

Cloudberry Mousse: Energy 501kcal/2082kJ; Protein 5.3g; Carbohydrate 30.8g, of which sugars 30.8g; Fat 38.8g, of which saturates 24.2g; Cholesterol 92mg; Calcium 63mg; Fibre 0.6g; Sodium 96mg.

Almond Biscuits: Energy 188kcal/788kJ; Protein 3.5g; Carbohydrate 22.5g, of which sugars 10.9g; Fat 10g, of which saturates 4.4g; Cholesterol 45mg; Calcium 44mg; Fibre 0.8g; Sodium 58mg.

Raspberry Jam Biscuits: Energy 711kcal/2992kJ; Protein 10.9g; Carbohydrate 110.7g, of which sugars 44.1g; Fat 28.1g, of which saturates 16.7g; Cholesterol 116mg; Calcium 173mg; Fibre 2.7g; Sodium 190mg.

Coffee Bread: Energy 1742kcal/7360kJ; Protein 42.5g; Carbohydrate 310.4g, of which sugars 81.8g; Fat 45.5g, of which saturates 24.3g; Cholesterol 345mg; Calcium 690mg; Fibre 9.3g; Sodium 1062mg.

Spice Cake: Energy 3379kcal/14025kJ; Protein 57.7g; Carbohydrate 191.1g, of which sugars 16.1g; Fat 271.1g, of which saturates 161.5g; Cholesterol 1421mg; Calcium 767mg; Fibre 7g; Sodium 1777mg.

Christmas Stars: Energy 155kcal/648kJ; Protein 1.5g; Carbohydrate 14.6g, of which sugars 7g; Fat 10.5g, of which saturates 6.5g; Cholesterol 27mg; Calcium 23mg; Fibre 1.5g; Sodium 78mg.

Runeberg's Cakes: Energy 370kcal/1551kJ; Protein 5.4g; Carbohydrate 43.2g, of which sugars 24.1g; Fat 19.2g, of which saturates 9.3g; Cholesterol 67mg; Calcium 68mg; Fibre 1.2g; Sodium 198mg.

Index